Current Economic Impact:

1. **Market Growth:**
    a. The global AI market has been experiencing exponential growth, with projections estimating it to reach trillions of dollars in value in the coming years.
2. **Job Creation and Transformation:**
    a. While AI is automating certain tasks, it is also creating new job categories and opportunities in AI development, data analysis, and related fields.
3. **Productivity and Efficiency:**
    a. AI is enhancing productivity by automating routine tasks, optimizing operations, and enabling data-driven decision-making.
4. **Industries Transformed by AI:**
    a. **Finance:** AI-driven trading algorithms, fraud detection, customer service chatbots.
    b. **Healthcare:** Diagnostic tools, patient monitoring systems, personalized medicine.
    c. **Retail:** Personalized recommendations, inventory management, supply chain optimization.
    d. **Manufacturing:** Predictive maintenance, quality control, robotics.
    e. **Transportation:** Autonomous vehicles, route optimization, traffic management.

Future Predictions:

1. **Economic Value Creation:**
    a. AI is expected to contribute significantly to global GDP growth, with some estimates suggesting an additional $15.7 trillion to the global economy by 2030.
2. **Workforce Evolution:**s
    a. The nature of work will continue to evolve, with a greater emphasis on skills in AI development, data science, and AI-human collaboration.
3. **Technological Advancements:**
    a. Continued advancements in AI research will lead to more sophisticated and capable AI systems, pushing the boundaries of what is possible.
4. **Ethical and Regulatory Considerations:**
    a. Governments and organizations will need to address ethical concerns and establish regulations to ensure the responsible development and use of AI.
5. **AI in Everyday Life:**
    a. AI will become increasingly integrated into daily life, from smart home devices to personalized education and beyond.

Conclusion

This chapter provides a foundational understanding of AI, its historical development, current technologies, and the profound economic impact it has today and will continue to have in the future. By exploring these aspects, readers can appreciate the vast potential of AI to drive profits and transform industries, setting the stage for the practical applications and strategies detailed in the subsequent chapters.

Overview of AI and Its Potential for Profit

Definition and Brief History of AI

Definition of AI: Artificial Intelligence (AI) refers to the simulation of human intelligence in machines that are programmed to think, learn, and make decisions. These machines can perform tasks that typically require human intelligence, such as visual perception, speech recognition, decision-making, and language translation.

Brief History of AI:

1. **1940s-1950s: Early Foundations**
   a. The concept of AI dates back to ancient times, but modern AI began to take shape with the invention of computers.
   b. Alan Turing's seminal 1950 paper, "Computing Machinery and Intelligence," posed the question, "Can machines think?" and introduced the Turing Test to evaluate machine intelligence.
2. **1956: The Dartmouth Conference**
   a. Often considered the birthplace of AI as a field, the Dartmouth Conference brought together key researchers who laid the groundwork for AI research.
3. **1960s-1970s: The First AI Winter**
   a. Initial excitement led to significant funding and early developments, such as the creation of the first AI programs and languages like LISP.
   b. However, progress was slower than expected, leading to reduced funding and interest, a period known as the "AI Winter."
4. **1980s: Expert Systems**
   a. Renewed interest in AI led to the development of expert systems, which used rule-based programming to mimic the decision-making of human experts.
   b. These systems found applications in industries like medicine and finance.
5. **1990s-2000s: Machine Learning and Data**
   a. Advances in computing power and the availability of large datasets spurred the development of machine learning algorithms.
   b. Notable achievements included IBM's Deep Blue defeating world chess champion Garry Kasparov in 1997.
6. **2010s-Present: Deep Learning and AI Boom**
   a. The advent of deep learning, a subset of machine learning involving neural networks with many layers, revolutionized AI capabilities.
   b. Breakthroughs in image and speech recognition, natural language processing, and autonomous systems marked this period.
   c. AI technologies became widely adopted across various sectors, leading to significant investments and research.

The Current State of AI Technology

Key Technologies and Applications:

1. **Machine Learning (ML)**:
   a. ML involves training algorithms on data to enable them to make predictions or decisions without being explicitly programmed.
   b. Applications: Spam detection, recommendation systems, predictive maintenance.
2. **Deep Learning**:
   a. A subset of ML, deep learning uses neural networks with many layers to model complex patterns in data.
   b. Applications: Image and speech recognition, natural language processing (NLP), autonomous driving.
3. **Natural Language Processing (NLP)**:
   a. NLP focuses on the interaction between computers and human language, enabling machines to understand, interpret, and generate human language.
   b. Applications: Chatbots, language translation, sentiment analysis.
4. **Computer Vision**:
   a. This field enables machines to interpret and make decisions based on visual input from the world.
   b. Applications: Facial recognition, medical imaging analysis, self-driving cars.
5. **Robotics**:
   a. AI-powered robots can perform tasks in a variety of environments, from manufacturing to healthcare.
   b. Applications: Industrial automation, surgical robots, drone technology.
6. **Reinforcement Learning**:
   a. A type of machine learning where agents learn to make decisions by receiving rewards or penalties for their actions.
   b. Applications: Game playing, autonomous navigation, resource management.

Current Trends and Developments:

1. **Edge AI**:
   a. AI processing is moving closer to the data source (edge devices) to reduce latency and improve real-time decision-making.
2. **AI Ethics and Fairness**:
   a. Growing awareness and research into ensuring AI systems are fair, transparent, and unbiased.
3. **AI in Healthcare**:
   a. Innovations in medical diagnostics, personalized treatment plans, and drug discovery.
4. **AI for Sustainability**:
   a. AI applications aimed at addressing environmental challenges, such as climate modeling and optimizing energy use.

The Economic Impact of AI and Future Predictions

Chapter 1: Understanding AI and Its Applications

Basics of AI and Machine Learning

What is AI?

1. **Definition**:
    a. AI, or Artificial Intelligence, is the field of computer science focused on creating systems capable of performing tasks that typically require human intelligence. This includes problem-solving, understanding natural language, recognizing patterns, and making decisions.
2. **Types of AI**:
    a. **Narrow AI**: Also known as Weak AI, this type is designed to perform a narrow task (e.g., facial recognition, internet searches, self-driving cars).
    b. **General AI**: Also known as Strong AI, this type can understand, learn, and apply knowledge in a way similar to human intelligence. It is still largely theoretical and not yet achieved.
    c. **Superintelligent AI**: This hypothetical type surpasses human intelligence and capabilities in all aspects. It remains a topic of speculation and debate.

How Machine Learning Works

1. **Definition**:
    a. Machine Learning (ML) is a subset of AI that involves training algorithms to make predictions or decisions based on data. Instead of being explicitly programmed for specific tasks, ML systems learn from data patterns and improve over time.
2. **Key Components**:
    a. **Data**: The foundation of ML, comprising the information used to train models.
    b. **Algorithms**: Mathematical models that process data and learn from it. Common algorithms include decision trees, support vector machines, and neural networks.
    c. **Training**: The process of feeding data to the algorithm to learn patterns. This often involves splitting data into training and testing sets.
    d. **Evaluation**: Assessing the performance of the model using metrics such as accuracy, precision, recall, and F1 score.
    e. **Prediction**: Once trained, the model can make predictions or decisions based on new, unseen data.

Key Terms and Concepts

1. **Neural Networks**: Inspired by the human brain, these are a series of algorithms that attempt to recognize underlying relationships in a set of data through a process that mimics the way the human brain operates.

2. **Deep Learning**: A subset of ML involving neural networks with many layers, enabling the model to learn from data in a hierarchical manner.
3. **Supervised Learning**: A type of ML where the model is trained on labeled data. The algorithm learns from the input-output pairs to predict outcomes on new data.
4. **Unsupervised Learning**: The model is trained on unlabeled data, aiming to find hidden patterns or intrinsic structures in the input data.
5. **Reinforcement Learning**: Involves training an agent to make a sequence of decisions by rewarding desired behaviors and/or punishing undesired ones.
6. **Overfitting and Underfitting**: Overfitting occurs when a model learns the training data too well, capturing noise and performing poorly on new data. Underfitting happens when the model is too simple to capture the underlying pattern of the data.
7. **Hyperparameters**: Parameters that are set before training a model and used to control the learning process (e.g., learning rate, batch size).

AI Tools and Technologies

Popular AI Platforms and Software

1. **TensorFlow**:
    a. Developed by Google, TensorFlow is an open-source platform for machine learning. It offers a comprehensive, flexible ecosystem of tools, libraries, and community resources for building and deploying ML models.
2. **PyTorch**:
    a. Developed by Facebook's AI Research lab, PyTorch is an open-source machine learning library based on the Torch library. It is known for its flexibility and ease of use, particularly for developing deep learning models.
3. **Scikit-Learn**:
    a. An open-source ML library for Python, Scikit-Learn features simple and efficient tools for data mining and data analysis, built on NumPy, SciPy, and matplotlib.
4. **Keras**:
    a. An open-source software library that provides a Python interface for artificial neural networks. Keras acts as an interface for the TensorFlow library.
5. **IBM Watson**:
    a. A suite of enterprise-ready AI services, applications, and tools. IBM Watson offers advanced NLP, ML, and automated AI lifecycle management.
6. **Amazon Web Services (AWS) AI Services**:
    a. AWS offers a range of AI services and infrastructure, including Amazon SageMaker, a fully managed service for building, training, and deploying machine learning models.
7. **Google AI Platform**:

a. Google's AI and ML products and services offer a suite of tools for building, deploying, and managing AI models, including AutoML, AI Platform, and TensorFlow Extended (TFX).

How to Choose the Right AI Tools for Your Needs

1. **Define Your Goals**:
   a. Identify the specific problems you want to solve with AI. This could be anything from automating repetitive tasks, enhancing customer experience, improving decision-making processes, or creating new products and services.
2. **Assess Your Resources**:
   a. Consider the available budget, the expertise of your team, and the computational resources required. Some tools are more user-friendly and require less specialized knowledge, while others might offer more advanced capabilities but need a higher level of expertise.
3. **Consider the Type of AI**:
   a. Choose tools that align with the type of AI you need (e.g., machine learning, deep learning, NLP, computer vision). Some platforms are better suited for specific types of AI.
4. **Evaluate Integration Capabilities**:
   a. Ensure the AI tools can integrate seamlessly with your existing systems and data sources. Look for compatibility with your current technology stack.
5. **Scalability and Flexibility**:
   a. Select tools that can scale with your needs. If you plan to expand your AI applications, choose platforms that can handle increased data volumes and more complex models.
6. **Community and Support**:
   a. Tools with active communities and robust support systems can be advantageous, offering a wealth of resources, tutorials, and forums for troubleshooting and learning.
7. **Trial and Experimentation**:
   a. Before committing, test a few options through free trials or limited-feature versions. Experiment with different tools to see which best meets your needs in terms of performance, usability, and results.

Conclusion

This chapter has laid the foundation for understanding AI and machine learning, including the essential concepts, key technologies, and popular tools available. By grasping these basics, readers are equipped with the knowledge to explore and apply AI effectively in various domains, paving the way for profitable ventures and innovations.

Chapter 2: AI-Powered E-commerce

Enhancing Customer Experience with AI

Personalized Recommendations

1. **Understanding Personalized Recommendations**:
   a. Personalized recommendations involve using AI algorithms to analyze customer behavior and preferences to suggest products or services tailored to individual customers.
2. **Techniques and Algorithms**:
   a. **Collaborative Filtering**: Recommends items by analyzing patterns and preferences of similar users.
   b. **Content-Based Filtering**: Suggests products based on the characteristics of items the customer has shown interest in.
   c. **Hybrid Systems**: Combine collaborative and content-based filtering to enhance recommendation accuracy.
3. **Implementation**:
   a. Collect and analyze customer data such as browsing history, purchase history, and demographic information.
   b. Utilize AI tools like recommendation engines (e.g., Amazon Personalize, Google Recommendations AI) to process data and generate personalized suggestions.
4. **Benefits**:
   a. Increases customer satisfaction and loyalty by providing relevant and interesting product suggestions.
   b. Boosts sales and average order value as customers are more likely to purchase recommended items.
5. **Case Studies**:
   a. Amazon's recommendation engine, which accounts for a significant portion of its revenue by suggesting products based on customer behavior.

Chatbots and Customer Service Automation

1. **Introduction to AI Chatbots**:
   a. AI chatbots are virtual assistants that use natural language processing (NLP) to interact with customers, answering queries and providing support.
2. **Benefits of Chatbots**:
   a. **24/7 Availability**: Provide round-the-clock customer support without the need for human intervention.
   b. **Cost-Effective**: Reduces the need for large customer service teams, lowering operational costs.
   c. **Instant Response**: Delivers quick answers to common questions, improving customer satisfaction.
3. **Key Technologies**:

a. **Natural Language Processing (NLP)**: Enables chatbots to understand and respond to human language.
   b. **Machine Learning**: Allows chatbots to learn from interactions and improve over time.
4. **Implementation**:
   a. Define the scope and functionality of the chatbot (e.g., answering FAQs, processing orders, providing product recommendations).
   b. Choose a chatbot platform (e.g., Microsoft Bot Framework, Dialogflow, IBM Watson Assistant) and integrate it with your e-commerce site.
   c. Continuously train and update the chatbot with new information and customer interaction data.
5. **Best Practices**:
   a. Ensure the chatbot has a friendly and helpful tone.
   b. Provide clear options for customers to escalate to human support if needed.
   c. Regularly review chatbot performance and make necessary adjustments to improve accuracy and user experience.

AI in Inventory Management

Predictive Analytics for Stock Management

1. **Understanding Predictive Analytics**:
   a. Predictive analytics uses historical data, machine learning algorithms, and statistical models to forecast future outcomes, such as product demand and inventory needs.
2. **Benefits**:
   a. **Optimized Stock Levels**: Prevents overstocking and stockouts by accurately predicting demand.
   b. **Cost Savings**: Reduces carrying costs and minimizes losses due to unsold inventory.
   c. **Improved Customer Satisfaction**: Ensures products are available when customers need them.
3. **Key Techniques**:
   a. **Time Series Analysis**: Analyzes data points collected or recorded at specific time intervals to predict future values.
   b. **Regression Analysis**: Identifies the relationship between variables to forecast future demand.
   c. **Machine Learning Models**: Utilize algorithms like random forests, neural networks, and gradient boosting for more accurate predictions.
4. **Implementation**:
   a. Collect historical sales data, seasonal trends, marketing campaigns, and external factors (e.g., economic indicators).
   b. Use predictive analytics tools (e.g., SAS Predictive Analytics, IBM SPSS, Microsoft Azure Machine Learning) to analyze the data and generate forecasts.
5. **Case Studies**:

a. Retail giants like Walmart and Target use predictive analytics to optimize inventory levels, reduce costs, and improve supply chain efficiency.

Automating Supply Chain Processes

1. **Introduction to Supply Chain Automation**:
   a. AI-driven automation in supply chain management involves using technology to streamline and optimize various processes, from procurement to delivery.
2. **Key Benefits**:
   a. **Increased Efficiency**: Reduces manual intervention, speeds up processes, and minimizes errors.
   b. **Cost Reduction**: Lowers operational costs by automating repetitive tasks.
   c. **Enhanced Visibility**: Provides real-time insights into supply chain operations, allowing for better decision-making.
3. **Key Technologies**:
   a. **Robotic Process Automation (RPA)**: Automates routine tasks such as order processing and invoicing.
   b. **AI and Machine Learning**: Optimize logistics, demand forecasting, and supplier management.
   c. **Internet of Things (IoT)**: Connects devices and systems across the supply chain for real-time data collection and monitoring.
4. **Implementation**:
   a. Identify processes that can benefit from automation (e.g., order fulfillment, inventory tracking, supplier communication).
   b. Choose appropriate automation tools and platforms (e.g., UiPath, Automation Anywhere, Blue Prism).
   c. Integrate automation solutions with existing systems and train staff to manage and monitor automated processes.
5. **Best Practices**:
   a. Ensure data accuracy and consistency across the supply chain.
   b. Continuously monitor and refine automated processes to adapt to changing business needs.
   c. Foster collaboration between human workers and automated systems to maximize efficiency and effectiveness.

Boosting Sales with AI

Dynamic Pricing Strategies

1. **Understanding Dynamic Pricing**:
   a. Dynamic pricing involves adjusting prices in real-time based on various factors such as demand, competition, and customer behavior.
2. **Benefits**:
   a. **Maximized Revenue**: Adjusts prices to capture higher margins during peak demand periods.

      b. **Competitive Advantage**: Responds quickly to market changes and competitor pricing.
      c. **Customer Segmentation**: Tailor prices based on customer segments and purchasing patterns.
3. **Key Techniques**:
      a. **Rule-Based Pricing**: Sets pricing rules based on predefined criteria (e.g., competitor prices, inventory levels).
      b. **Algorithmic Pricing**: Uses machine learning algorithms to analyze data and make pricing decisions.
      c. **Price Elasticity Analysis**: Measures how sensitive customers are to price changes and adjusts prices accordingly.
4. **Implementation**:
      a. Collect and analyze data on customer behavior, competitor pricing, and market trends.
      b. Use dynamic pricing tools (e.g., Prisync, RepricerExpress, Dynamic Pricing by Omnia) to automate price adjustments.
      c. Continuously monitor pricing performance and make necessary adjustments to optimize results.
5. **Case Studies**:
      a. Companies like Uber and Airbnb use dynamic pricing to adjust rates based on demand, leading to increased revenue and market responsiveness.

AI-Driven Marketing and Ad Targeting

1. **Introduction to AI-Driven Marketing**:
      a. AI-driven marketing leverages machine learning and data analytics to create personalized and effective marketing campaigns.
2. **Benefits**:
      a. **Personalized Campaigns**: Tailors marketing messages to individual customer preferences and behaviors.
      b. **Improved ROI**: Optimizes ad spend by targeting the right audience with relevant content.
      c. **Enhanced Customer Insights**: Provides deep insights into customer behavior and preferences.
3. **Key Techniques**:
      a. **Customer Segmentation**: Uses AI to group customers based on similar characteristics and behaviors for targeted marketing.
      b. **Predictive Analytics**: Forecasts customer behavior and identifies high-value prospects.
      c. **Natural Language Processing (NLP)**: Analyzes customer sentiment and feedback to refine marketing strategies.
4. **Implementation**:
      a. Collect and analyze customer data from various sources (e.g., website analytics, social media, CRM systems).
      b. Use AI marketing platforms (e.g., HubSpot, Marketo, Salesforce Einstein) to automate and optimize marketing campaigns.

      c. Continuously monitor campaign performance and adjust strategies based on data-driven insights.
5. **Best Practices**:
      a. Ensure data privacy and compliance with regulations (e.g., GDPR, CCPA).
      b. Foster a data-driven culture within the marketing team to maximize the benefits of AI tools.
      c. Regularly update and refine AI models to keep up with changing customer preferences and market trends.

Conclusion

This chapter has explored the various ways AI can enhance e-commerce operations, from improving customer experience through personalized recommendations and chatbots, to optimizing inventory management and boosting sales with dynamic pricing and AI-driven marketing. By leveraging these AI-powered strategies, e-commerce businesses can increase efficiency, reduce costs, and ultimately drive higher revenue and customer satisfaction.

Chapter 3: AI-Powered Side Hustles

Freelancing with AI Tools

Using AI for Graphic Design, Writing, and More

1. **Graphic Design**:
   a. **AI Tools**:
      i. Canva: Offers AI-powered design suggestions, layouts, and templates.
      ii. Adobe Sensei: Integrates AI to automate repetitive tasks and provide design recommendations.
   b. **Applications**:
      i. Creating logos, social media graphics, and marketing materials.
      ii. Automating photo editing and enhancement tasks.
2. **Writing**:
   a. **AI Tools**:
      i. Grammarly: Provides grammar and style suggestions using AI.
      ii. Jasper: Generates content based on prompts, aiding in blog writing, ad copy, and social media posts.
   b. **Applications**:
      i. Crafting articles, blog posts, and marketing copy.
      ii. Editing and proofreading for clients to ensure polished final drafts.
3. **Video and Audio Editing**:
   a. **AI Tools**:
      i. Descript: Transcribes audio and video, allowing for easy editing via text interface.
      ii. Adobe Premiere Pro: Uses AI to enhance video editing capabilities, including automated scene selection and color correction.
   b. **Applications**:
      i. Creating promotional videos, podcasts, and webinars.
      ii. Automating tasks like noise reduction, audio leveling, and subtitle generation.

Platforms that Offer AI-Powered Freelance Opportunities

1. **Freelance Marketplaces**:
   a. **Upwork**: Features job listings for AI-driven services like content creation, design, and data analysis.
   b. **Fiverr**: Allows freelancers to offer AI-powered services such as chatbot development, AI-generated art, and automated marketing solutions.
2. **Specialized Platforms**:
   a. **Toptal**: Connects businesses with top freelancers skilled in AI and machine learning.
   b. **Freelancer.com**: Hosts projects specifically requiring AI expertise, from developing predictive models to creating automated systems.

Creating and Selling AI Products

Developing AI-Driven Apps and Software

1. **Identifying Opportunities**:
   a. Look for gaps in the market where AI can provide innovative solutions or improve existing processes.
   b. Example: Developing a personal finance app that uses AI to analyze spending patterns and offer budgeting advice.
2. **Tools and Technologies**:
   a. **Frameworks**: TensorFlow, PyTorch for building AI models.
   b. **Platforms**: AWS, Google Cloud AI for deploying and scaling AI applications.
3. **Development Process**:
   a. **Idea and Market Research**: Identify a problem that can be solved with AI, research the market demand, and validate the idea.
   b. **Prototyping**: Develop a minimum viable product (MVP) using AI tools and frameworks.
   c. **Testing and Iteration**: Continuously test the app with real users and refine it based on feedback.
   d. **Launch and Marketing**: Release the app on platforms like the Apple App Store, Google Play, or as a web application, and use AI-driven marketing tools to reach your target audience.

Monetizing AI-Generated Content (e.g., Art, Music, Writing)

1. **AI Art**:
   a. Use AI tools like DeepArt, Artbreeder, or DALL-E to create unique artworks.
   b. Sell digital prints on platforms like Etsy, Redbubble, or through your own website.
2. **AI Music**:
   a. Leverage AI music composition tools such as Amper Music, AIVA, or Jukedeck.
   b. Monetize by selling tracks on stock music sites, streaming platforms, or offering custom compositions for content creators.
3. **AI Writing**:
   a. Utilize AI writing tools like Jasper, ChatGPT, or Copysmith to generate articles, stories, and marketing content.
   b. Publish and monetize content through blogs, e-books, or freelance writing gigs.

Online Courses and Consulting

Teaching AI Skills

1. **Course Creation**:

a. Identify in-demand AI skills such as machine learning, data analysis, or natural language processing.
   b. Use platforms like Teachable, Udemy, or Coursera to create and sell courses.
   c. Develop comprehensive courses that include video lessons, hands-on projects, quizzes, and downloadable resources.
2. **Marketing Your Course**:
   a. Use AI-driven marketing tools to target potential students through personalized ads and email campaigns.
   b. Leverage social media, blogs, and webinars to promote your courses and engage with your audience.
3. **Monetization**:
   a. Offer tiered pricing models, including basic, premium, and personalized coaching options.
   b. Provide subscription-based access for continuous learning and updates.

Consulting on AI Implementation

1. **Identifying Clients**:
   a. Target businesses looking to implement AI solutions to improve operations, customer service, or product offerings.
   b. Network through professional platforms like LinkedIn or AI-focused industry groups to find potential clients.
2. **Consulting Services**:
   a. Offer services such as AI strategy development, project management, and implementation support.
   b. Provide training and workshops to help businesses understand and integrate AI technologies.
3. **Monetization Strategies**:
   a. Charge hourly rates, project-based fees, or retainer agreements based on the scope and complexity of the consulting work.
   b. Develop long-term partnerships with clients to offer ongoing support and updates.

Conclusion

In this chapter, we've explored various AI-powered side hustles, from freelancing with AI tools to creating and selling AI products, and offering online courses and consulting services. By leveraging AI technologies, individuals can tap into lucrative opportunities, enhance their skill sets, and generate additional income streams. With the right approach and tools, AI can transform side hustles into thriving businesses.

Chapter 4: AI in Digital Marketing

Optimizing Marketing Campaigns with AI

Using AI for Audience Segmentation and Targeting

1. **Audience Segmentation**:
   a. **Definition**: Audience segmentation involves dividing your target market into distinct groups based on various characteristics such as demographics, behavior, and interests.
   b. **AI Techniques**:
      i. **Clustering Algorithms**: Use algorithms like K-means or hierarchical clustering to group customers based on similarities in their data.
      ii. **Predictive Analytics**: Leverage historical data to predict which segments are most likely to respond to specific marketing efforts.
   c. **Benefits**:
      i. **Improved Targeting**: More accurate targeting leads to higher engagement and conversion rates.
      ii. **Increased ROI**: Optimize ad spend by focusing resources on high-value segments.
   d. **Implementation**:
      i. Collect data from various sources such as website analytics, social media, and CRM systems.
      ii. Use AI tools (e.g., HubSpot, Segment, BlueConic) to analyze data and create actionable segments.
      iii. Tailor marketing campaigns to the needs and preferences of each segment.

Personalizing Marketing Messages at Scale

1. **Personalization Techniques**:
   a. **Dynamic Content**: Use AI to automatically customize website content, email campaigns, and ads based on user behavior and preferences.
   b. **Behavioral Targeting**: Employ machine learning models to predict customer needs and deliver personalized recommendations in real time.
   c. **Natural Language Generation (NLG)**: Generate personalized email subject lines, product descriptions, and ad copy.
   d. **Benefits**:
      i. **Enhanced Customer Experience**: Personalization increases relevance and engagement, leading to improved customer satisfaction.
      ii. **Higher Conversion Rates**: Tailored messages drive higher conversion rates by addressing individual customer needs.
   e. **Implementation**:

i. Integrate AI-powered personalization tools (e.g., Dynamic Yield, Evergage, Optimizely) into your marketing platforms.
   ii. Continuously test and refine personalization strategies based on performance data.

Content Creation and Curation

AI Tools for Generating and Curating Content

1. **Content Generation**:
   a. **AI Writing Assistants**:
      i. **Examples**: Jasper (formerly Jarvis), Copy.ai, and Writesonic.
      ii. **Capabilities**: Generate blog posts, product descriptions, ad copy, and more based on prompts and keywords.
   b. **AI Art and Design**:
      i. **Examples**: DALL-E, Artbreeder, Runway ML.
      ii. **Capabilities**: Create unique visual content such as graphics, illustrations, and marketing materials.
   c. **Benefits**:
      i. **Time Savings**: Automate content creation to free up time for strategic tasks.
      ii. **Consistency**: Maintain a consistent brand voice and style across all content.
   d. **Implementation**:
      i. Define content needs and select appropriate AI tools.
      ii. Integrate AI-generated content into your content management system (CMS) and marketing channels.
2. **Content Curation**:
   a. **AI Tools**:
      i. **Examples**: Curata, Feedly, UpContent.
      ii. **Capabilities**: Aggregate and recommend relevant content based on user interests and industry trends.
   b. **Benefits**:
      i. **Enhanced Engagement**: Provide valuable and relevant content to your audience.
      ii. **Efficiency**: Automate the content curation process to stay current with industry trends and news.
   c. **Implementation**:
      i. Set up content curation tools to automatically gather and recommend content.
      ii. Use insights to inform content strategies and share curated content through your channels.

Enhancing SEO with AI

1. **AI for SEO Optimization**:
   a. **Keyword Research**:

            i. **Tools**: Ahrefs, SEMrush, Moz.
            ii. **Capabilities**: Identify high-value keywords and optimize content for search engine visibility.
        b. **On-Page SEO**:
            i. **Tools**: Clearscope, SurferSEO.
            ii. **Capabilities**: Analyze and optimize on-page elements like headings, meta descriptions, and keyword density.
        c. **Content Optimization**:
            i. **AI Tools**: Frase, MarketMuse.
            ii. **Capabilities**: Provide recommendations for improving content relevance and quality based on competitor analysis and search intent.
        d. **Benefits**:
            i. **Improved Rankings**: Boost search engine rankings by aligning content with search engine algorithms.
            ii. **Increased Traffic**: Drive more organic traffic to your website through optimized content.
        e. **Implementation**:
            i. Use AI-powered SEO tools to conduct audits, track performance, and make data-driven optimizations.
            ii. Continuously monitor and adjust SEO strategies based on insights and changes in search algorithms.

Social Media and Influencer Marketing

AI for Social Media Management and Analysis

1. **Social Media Management**:
    a. **AI Tools**:
        i. **Examples**: Hootsuite Insights, Buffer Analyze, Socialbakers.
        ii. **Capabilities**: Automate social media posting, analyze engagement, and track brand mentions.
    b. **Benefits**:
        i. **Efficiency**: Streamline social media management tasks and improve responsiveness.
        ii. **Insights**: Gain valuable insights into audience behavior, trends, and content performance.
    c. **Implementation**:
        i. Integrate AI tools into your social media management workflow.
        ii. Use analytics to inform content strategies and optimize social media campaigns.
2. **Social Media Analysis**:
    a. **AI Tools**:
        i. **Examples**: Brandwatch, Talkwalker, Sprout Social.
        ii. **Capabilities**: Analyze sentiment, identify trends, and monitor competitors.
    b. **Benefits**:

i. **Informed Decisions**: Make data-driven decisions based on comprehensive social media insights.
   ii. **Enhanced Strategy**: Adjust social media strategies based on performance metrics and trends.
   c. **Implementation**:
      i. Use AI-powered analytics tools to track and analyze social media performance.
      ii. Regularly review reports and adjust strategies to maximize engagement and impact.

Identifying and Partnering with Influencers Using AI

1. **Influencer Identification**:
   a. **AI Tools**:
      i. **Examples**: Traackr, Influencity, Klear.
      ii. **Capabilities**: Identify and evaluate influencers based on audience demographics, engagement metrics, and content relevance.
   b. **Benefits**:
      i. **Targeted Partnerships**: Find influencers who align with your brand and target audience.
      ii. **Data-Driven Decisions**: Make informed decisions about influencer collaborations based on performance data.
   c. **Implementation**:
      i. Use AI tools to search for and analyze potential influencers.
      ii. Assess influencer fit based on metrics such as reach, engagement, and audience demographics.
2. **Partnership Management**:
   a. **AI Tools**:
      i. **Examples**: AspireIQ, Upfluence, Influencer.co.
      ii. **Capabilities**: Manage influencer campaigns, track performance, and measure ROI.
   b. **Benefits**:
      i. **Streamlined Collaboration**: Manage influencer relationships and campaigns more efficiently.
      ii. **Performance Tracking**: Monitor campaign performance and adjust strategies based on insights.
   c. **Implementation**:
      i. Set up AI-powered influencer management tools to track campaign progress and results.
      ii. Analyze performance metrics and collaborate with influencers to optimize campaign effectiveness.

Conclusion

This chapter has delved into how AI can transform digital marketing efforts by optimizing campaigns, enhancing content creation and SEO, and leveraging social media and influencer partnerships. By incorporating AI tools and strategies, businesses can improve targeting, personalization, and overall marketing effectiveness, leading to better engagement, higher conversion rates, and increased revenue.

Chapter 5: AI in Stock Market and Trading

Automated Trading Systems

Overview of AI-Driven Trading Bots

1. **Definition and Functionality**:
   a. **AI Trading Bots**: Automated systems that use artificial intelligence to execute trades on behalf of investors based on predefined criteria and real-time data analysis.
   b. **How They Work**: AI trading bots analyze market data, identify trading opportunities, and execute trades according to programmed algorithms or machine learning models.
2. **Types of Trading Bots**:
   a. **Algorithmic Trading Bots**:
      i. **Examples**: Market makers, statistical arbitrage bots.
      ii. **Function**: Use predefined algorithms to execute trades based on historical data and statistical models.
   b. **Sentiment Analysis Bots**:
      i. **Examples**: Bots that analyze news sentiment and social media trends.
      ii. **Function**: Monitor and interpret market sentiment to inform trading decisions.
   c. **High-Frequency Trading Bots**:
      i. **Examples**: Bots designed for rapid, high-frequency trades to capitalize on short-term market movements.
      ii. **Function**: Execute a large number of trades at extremely high speeds, often exploiting small price discrepancies.
3. **Benefits**:
   a. **24/7 Trading**: Bots can operate around the clock, taking advantage of trading opportunities in different time zones.
   b. **Emotion-Free Trading**: Automated systems execute trades based on data, reducing the impact of emotional decision-making.
   c. **Efficiency**: Bots can process and act on vast amounts of market data faster than human traders.
4. **Challenges**:
   a. **Technical Issues**: Bots may experience glitches or failures that can impact trading performance.
   b. **Over-Reliance on Algorithms**: Bots may perform poorly in volatile or unprecedented market conditions if not properly calibrated.

Setting Up and Optimizing Automated Trading Strategies

1. **Choosing a Trading Platform**:
   a. **Platforms**: MetaTrader 4/5, Tradestation, NinjaTrader.

    b. **Considerations**: Evaluate features such as backtesting capabilities, integration with AI tools, and support for different asset classes.
2. **Developing a Trading Strategy**:
    a. **Strategy Types**:
        i. **Trend Following**: Algorithms that identify and capitalize on market trends.
        ii. **Mean Reversion**: Strategies that bet on the return of prices to their historical averages.
        iii. **Momentum Trading**: Bots that focus on stocks or assets experiencing significant price movement.
    b. **Backtesting**: Test your trading strategy on historical data to evaluate its effectiveness and refine parameters.
3. **Optimization**:
    a. **Parameter Tuning**: Adjust trading parameters (e.g., stop-loss, take-profit levels) to improve performance.
    b. **Performance Metrics**: Monitor metrics such as win rate, Sharpe ratio, and maximum drawdown to assess and optimize performance.
    c. **Continuous Monitoring**: Regularly review and adjust strategies based on market conditions and trading outcomes.

Predictive Analytics for Investment

Using AI to Forecast Market Trends

1. **Introduction to Predictive Analytics**:
    a. **Definition**: Predictive analytics involves using statistical algorithms and machine learning techniques to forecast future market trends based on historical data.
    b. **Data Sources**: Includes historical stock prices, economic indicators, market news, and social media sentiment.
2. **AI Techniques**:
    a. **Time Series Analysis**:
        i. **Models**: ARIMA (AutoRegressive Integrated Moving Average), LSTM (Long Short-Term Memory).
        ii. **Application**: Analyze historical price data to predict future price movements and trends.
    b. **Machine Learning Models**:
        i. **Examples**: Random Forests, Gradient Boosting Machines, Neural Networks.
        ii. **Application**: Train models on historical market data to forecast future trends and trading signals.
    c. **Sentiment Analysis**:
        i. **Tools**: Natural Language Processing (NLP) algorithms to analyze news articles, social media, and financial reports.
        ii. **Application**: Gauge market sentiment and its potential impact on asset prices.
3. **Benefits**:

a. **Enhanced Accuracy**: Improve forecasting accuracy by leveraging complex algorithms and large datasets.
   b. **Timely Insights**: Obtain actionable insights to make informed investment decisions and adjust strategies promptly.
4. **Challenges**:
   a. **Model Overfitting**: Risk of models becoming too tailored to historical data and failing to generalize to new market conditions.
   b. **Data Quality**: Reliance on accurate and high-quality data for effective predictions.

Risk Management with AI

1. **Introduction to AI-Driven Risk Management**:
   a. **Definition**: Using AI to identify, assess, and mitigate risks associated with investments and trading.
   b. **Importance**: Effective risk management helps protect investments from significant losses and enhances overall portfolio stability.
2. **AI Techniques for Risk Management**:
   a. **Risk Prediction Models**:
      i. **Examples**: Value at Risk (VaR) models, Conditional Value at Risk (CVaR), Stress Testing.
      ii. **Application**: Predict potential losses and assess the impact of extreme market conditions.
   b. **Portfolio Optimization**:
      i. **Tools**: Modern Portfolio Theory (MPT), Mean-Variance Optimization.
      ii. **Application**: Optimize portfolio allocation to balance risk and return.
   c. **Fraud Detection**:
      i. **AI Tools**: Anomaly detection algorithms to identify suspicious trading patterns and potential fraud.
      ii. **Application**: Enhance security and prevent fraudulent activities in trading.
3. **Benefits**:
   a. **Proactive Management**: Identify and mitigate risks before they materialize, reducing potential losses.
   b. **Enhanced Decision-Making**: Make more informed decisions based on data-driven insights and risk assessments.
4. **Challenges**:
   a. **Complexity**: Developing and maintaining effective AI-driven risk management systems can be complex and resource-intensive.
   b. **Data Dependencies**: Dependence on high-quality data and accurate modeling for effective risk management.

Robo-Advisors

Benefits and Limitations of AI-Driven Investment Advisors

1. **Benefits**:
    a. **Cost-Effectiveness**: Lower fees compared to traditional financial advisors due to automation and reduced need for human intervention.
    b. **Accessibility**: Provides investment advice and portfolio management to a broader audience, including those with lower investment amounts.
    c. **Consistency**: Automated systems offer consistent and disciplined investment strategies without emotional bias.
    d. **Customization**: Many robo-advisors use AI to tailor investment recommendations based on individual risk tolerance, financial goals, and preferences.
2. **Limitations**:
    a. **Lack of Human Touch**: Limited ability to offer personalized advice and address complex financial situations that may require human judgment.
    b. **Algorithm Limitations**: Performance depends on the algorithms used and may not account for all market conditions or external factors.
    c. **Data Security**: Potential risks related to the security of personal and financial data stored and processed by robo-advisors.

Selecting the Right Robo-Advisor for Your Needs

1. **Key Factors to Consider**:
    a. **Investment Goals and Risk Tolerance**: Choose a robo-advisor that aligns with your financial goals, risk tolerance, and investment preferences.
    b. **Fees and Costs**: Evaluate fee structures, including management fees, trading fees, and any additional costs associated with the service.
    c. **Features and Services**: Look for additional features such as tax-loss harvesting, retirement planning, and access to human advisors if needed.
    d. **Reputation and Reviews**: Research the robo-advisor's reputation, user reviews, and track record to ensure reliability and performance.
2. **Popular Robo-Advisors**:
    a. **Examples**: Betterment, Wealthfront, Charles Schwab Intelligent Portfolios.
    b. **Comparison**: Review and compare services, fees, and features to select the best option for your investment needs.

Conclusion

In this chapter, we have explored the various applications of AI in the stock market and trading. From automated trading systems and predictive analytics to robo-advisors, AI is transforming the way investors approach the financial markets. By leveraging AI tools and techniques, traders and investors can enhance their decision-making, optimize strategies, and manage risks more effectively. However, it is crucial to understand both the benefits and limitations of AI-driven approaches to maximize their potential and achieve successful investment outcomes.

Chapter 6: AI in Real Estate

AI for Property Valuation

Using AI to Assess Property Values and Trends

1. **AI-Powered Valuation Models**:
   a. **Definition and Importance**: AI-driven valuation models use machine learning algorithms to estimate property values based on a wide range of data inputs, such as historical sales data, market trends, and property characteristics.
   b. **Functionality**:
      i. **Data Integration**: Aggregates data from public records, real estate listings, economic indicators, and geographic information systems (GIS).
      ii. **Algorithmic Analysis**: Uses algorithms to identify patterns and predict future price trends.
   c. **Advantages**:
      i. **Accuracy**: Provides more accurate and up-to-date valuations compared to traditional methods.
      ii. **Speed**: Delivers quick assessments, helping buyers, sellers, and investors make informed decisions faster.
      iii. **Scalability**: Can analyze large volumes of data across multiple properties and regions.
2. **Key Factors Considered in AI Valuation**:
   a. **Property Characteristics**: Size, age, type, and condition of the property.
   b. **Location Attributes**: Proximity to schools, transportation, and amenities.
   c. **Market Conditions**: Supply and demand dynamics, economic growth, and interest rates.

Tools for Real-Time Market Analysis

1. **AI-Powered Market Analysis Tools**:
   a. **Platforms**: Zillow's Zestimate, Redfin's Price Estimate, HouseCanary.
   b. **Features**:
      i. **Data Visualization**: Interactive charts and maps to visualize market trends.
      ii. **Predictive Analytics**: Forecasts future market movements and property values.
      iii. **Comparative Analysis**: Compares similar properties to determine fair market value.
   c. **Benefits**:
      i. **Informed Decision-Making**: Provides stakeholders with data-driven insights for buying, selling, and investing.

ii. **Competitive Advantage**: Identifies emerging trends and opportunities in the market.
   d. **Implementation**:
      i. **Subscription Services**: Access platforms that offer comprehensive market analysis tools.
      ii. **Custom Solutions**: Develop tailored AI solutions to meet specific business needs and objectives.

Enhancing Property Management

AI-Driven Tenant Screening and Management

1. **Tenant Screening Process**:
   a. **AI Tools**:
      i. **Examples**: RentPrep, Cozy, TenantCloud.
      ii. **Functionality**: Evaluate tenant applications, assess creditworthiness, and conduct background checks.
   b. **Benefits**:
      i. **Efficiency**: Streamlines the screening process, reducing time and administrative burden.
      ii. **Accuracy**: Enhances decision-making by analyzing a wider range of data points, including rental history, employment status, and financial behavior.
      iii. **Risk Mitigation**: Reduces the risk of selecting unreliable tenants and potential disputes.
2. **Tenant Management Solutions**:
   a. **AI Features**:
      i. **Automated Communication**: Chatbots and AI-driven communication systems for tenant inquiries and support.
      ii. **Lease Management**: Automate lease agreements, renewals, and rent collection.
   b. **Benefits**:
      i. **Enhanced Tenant Experience**: Provides timely and consistent responses to tenant requests and issues.
      ii. **Operational Efficiency**: Reduces manual workload and streamlines management tasks.

Predictive Maintenance Using AI

1. **Predictive Maintenance in Real Estate**:
   a. **Definition and Benefits**: AI-driven predictive maintenance uses data and machine learning to anticipate maintenance needs, minimizing downtime and costs.
   b. **How It Works**:
      i. **Data Collection**: Gathers data from IoT sensors, maintenance logs, and building systems.

ii. **Analysis**: AI algorithms analyze data to predict equipment failures and schedule maintenance proactively.
    c. **Benefits**:
        i. **Cost Savings**: Reduces repair costs by addressing issues before they escalate.
        ii. **Efficiency**: Optimizes maintenance schedules, minimizing disruptions to tenants.
        iii. **Longevity**: Extends the life of building systems and equipment.
2. **Tools and Technologies**:
    a. **AI Platforms**: IBM Maximo, SAP Predictive Maintenance, Building Engines.
    b. **Implementation**:
        i. **Integration**: Incorporate AI-driven maintenance solutions into property management systems.
        ii. **Monitoring**: Use real-time data to continuously monitor building health and performance.

Marketing Real Estate with AI

Virtual Tours and AI-Enhanced Property Listings

1. **Virtual Tours**:
    a. **Definition and Importance**: Virtual tours provide a 360-degree view of properties, allowing potential buyers and tenants to explore spaces remotely.
    b. **AI Tools**:
        i. **Examples**: Matterport, Zillow 3D Home, EyeSpy360.
        ii. **Capabilities**: Create interactive, immersive experiences with high-resolution images and videos.
    c. **Benefits**:
        i. **Increased Engagement**: Attracts more interest by offering an in-depth view of properties.
        ii. **Broader Reach**: Enables remote viewing, appealing to international buyers or those unable to visit in person.
2. **AI-Enhanced Property Listings**:
    a. **Features**:
        i. **Optimized Descriptions**: Use AI to generate compelling and accurate property descriptions.
        ii. **Image Enhancement**: AI tools enhance listing photos to showcase properties in the best light.
        iii. **SEO Optimization**: Improves search engine visibility through AI-driven keyword strategies.
    b. **Implementation**:
        i. **Integration**: Utilize AI tools to create and manage property listings across multiple platforms.
        ii. **Promotion**: Leverage AI insights to tailor marketing strategies and reach target audiences effectively.

Targeted Advertising for Real Estate

1. **AI-Powered Advertising Strategies**:
   a. **Definition**: AI-driven advertising involves creating and delivering personalized ads to specific audience segments based on data analysis.
   b. **Tools and Platforms**:
      i. **Examples**: Facebook Ads, Google Ads, AdRoll.
      ii. **Capabilities**: Analyze user behavior, demographics, and preferences to tailor ad content.
   c. **Benefits**:
      i. **Higher ROI**: Increases ad effectiveness by reaching the right audience with relevant messages.
      ii. **Better Engagement**: Enhances click-through rates and conversions by delivering personalized ads.
2. **Implementation Strategies**:
   a. **Audience Segmentation**: Use AI to identify and target specific buyer personas and demographics.
   b. **Content Personalization**: Tailor ad content and messaging to match audience interests and preferences.
   c. **Performance Monitoring**: Continuously analyze ad performance data to refine and optimize strategies.

Conclusion

In this chapter, we have explored the transformative impact of AI in the real estate industry. From AI-driven property valuation and market analysis to advanced property management and targeted marketing, AI technologies are revolutionizing how real estate professionals operate and interact with clients. By embracing these innovative tools and strategies, real estate businesses can enhance efficiency, accuracy, and customer satisfaction, ultimately achieving greater success in a competitive market.

Chapter 7: AI for Entrepreneurs and Small Businesses

Introduction

1. **The Role of AI in Business Transformation**:
   a. **Overview**: AI is revolutionizing the way entrepreneurs and small businesses operate by offering innovative solutions to streamline processes, enhance decision-making, and improve customer relationships.
   b. **Significance**: AI technology empowers small businesses to compete with larger corporations by leveraging automation and data-driven insights.

AI for Business Operations

Streamlining Operations with AI Automation

1. **AI Automation Overview**:
   a. **Definition**: AI automation involves using machine learning algorithms and robotic process automation (RPA) to perform repetitive tasks, reduce human intervention, and enhance operational efficiency.
   b. **Applications**:
      i. **Process Automation**: Automating routine tasks such as data entry, invoice processing, and scheduling.
      ii. **Supply Chain Management**: Enhancing inventory management, demand forecasting, and logistics planning.
   c. **Benefits**:
      i. **Cost Savings**: Reduces labor costs by automating manual tasks.
      ii. **Efficiency**: Increases productivity and accuracy by minimizing human error.
      iii. **Scalability**: Enables businesses to handle increased workloads without additional resources.
2. **Implementation**:
   a. **Identify Opportunities**: Conduct a thorough analysis of existing processes to identify automation opportunities.
   b. **Select Tools**: Choose AI and RPA tools that align with business needs, such as UiPath, Blue Prism, and Automation Anywhere.
   c. **Integration**: Seamlessly integrate AI solutions into existing workflows to enhance overall efficiency.

Enhancing Decision-Making with AI Analytics

1. **AI Analytics Overview**:
   a. **Definition**: AI analytics involves using advanced data analysis techniques, such as machine learning and predictive modeling, to extract insights from large datasets.
   b. **Applications**:

            i. **Data Visualization**: Using AI-powered tools to create interactive dashboards and visualizations.
            ii. **Predictive Analytics**: Forecasting trends and identifying potential challenges based on historical data.
        c. **Benefits**:
            i. **Informed Decisions**: Provides data-driven insights that enable entrepreneurs to make strategic decisions.
            ii. **Risk Mitigation**: Identifies potential risks and opportunities, allowing for proactive planning.
            iii. **Competitive Advantage**: Leverages insights to gain an edge over competitors by anticipating market trends.
2. **Implementation**:
    a. **Data Collection**: Gather relevant data from various sources, including customer interactions, sales transactions, and market research.
    b. **Select Tools**: Utilize AI analytics platforms such as Google Analytics, Tableau, and Power BI.
    c. **Data Analysis**: Employ machine learning models to uncover patterns and generate actionable insights.

Customer Relationship Management (CRM)

AI-Powered CRM Systems for Small Businesses

1. **AI CRM Overview**:
    a. **Definition**: AI-powered CRM systems leverage artificial intelligence to automate and enhance customer relationship management tasks, such as lead scoring, customer segmentation, and communication.
    b. **Applications**:
        i. **Lead Management**: Automating lead scoring and nurturing processes to identify high-potential prospects.
        ii. **Customer Segmentation**: Grouping customers based on behavior, preferences, and demographics for targeted marketing.
    c. **Benefits**:
        i. **Improved Efficiency**: Automates routine CRM tasks, freeing up time for more strategic activities.
        ii. **Enhanced Customer Insights**: Provides deeper insights into customer behavior and preferences.
        iii. **Personalized Engagement**: Enables businesses to deliver personalized interactions and offers to customers.
2. **Implementation**:
    a. **Select CRM Tools**: Choose AI-driven CRM platforms like Salesforce Einstein, HubSpot, and Zoho CRM.
    b. **Data Integration**: Integrate customer data from various touchpoints to create a unified view of each customer.
    c. **AI Features**: Leverage AI features such as chatbots, predictive lead scoring, and sentiment analysis.

Personalizing Customer Interactions with AI

1. **Personalization Overview:**
   a. **Definition**: Personalization involves using AI to tailor interactions and communications based on individual customer preferences and behaviors.
   b. **Applications**:
      i. **Recommendation Engines**: Suggesting products or services based on past purchases and browsing behavior.
      ii. **Dynamic Content**: Delivering personalized content through email campaigns and websites.
   c. **Benefits**:
      i. **Customer Satisfaction**: Enhances the customer experience by delivering relevant and timely interactions.
      ii. **Increased Loyalty**: Builds stronger relationships with customers through personalized engagement.
      iii. **Higher Conversion Rates**: Improves conversion rates by delivering targeted offers and recommendations.
2. **Implementation**:
   a. **Data Collection**: Gather customer data from various touchpoints, such as website interactions and purchase history.
   b. **AI Tools**: Use AI-powered personalization platforms like Dynamic Yield, Monetate, and Segment.
   c. **Content Strategy**: Develop a personalization strategy that aligns with customer preferences and business goals.

Scaling Your Business with AI

Identifying Growth Opportunities Using AI

1. **AI-Driven Market Analysis:**
   a. **Definition**: Using AI to analyze market trends, customer behavior, and competitive dynamics to identify growth opportunities.
   b. **Applications**:
      i. **Market Research**: Gaining insights into emerging trends and consumer preferences.
      ii. **Competitive Analysis**: Monitoring competitors and identifying gaps in the market.
   c. **Benefits**:
      i. **Strategic Planning**: Provides data-driven insights for strategic business planning and expansion.
      ii. **Opportunity Identification**: Identifies untapped markets and potential areas for growth.
      iii. **Risk Assessment**: Assesses risks and challenges associated with growth initiatives.
2. **Implementation**:
   a. **Data Sources**: Utilize data from social media, online reviews, and market reports.

    b. **AI Tools**: Leverage AI market analysis platforms like SEMrush, SimilarWeb, and NetBase Quid.
    c. **Actionable Insights**: Translate AI insights into actionable strategies for business growth.

Implementing AI Solutions to Scale Efficiently

1. **AI for Scalability**:
    a. **Definition**: Implementing AI solutions to efficiently scale operations, optimize resource allocation, and support business growth.
    b. **Applications**:
        i. **Resource Optimization**: Using AI to allocate resources efficiently, such as staff scheduling and inventory management.
        ii. **Process Automation**: Scaling operations by automating repetitive tasks and processes.
    c. **Benefits**:
        i. **Scalable Infrastructure**: Enables businesses to handle increased demand without sacrificing quality or service.
        ii. **Cost Efficiency**: Reduces operational costs by optimizing resource allocation and minimizing waste.
        iii. **Adaptability**: Provides the flexibility to adapt to changing market conditions and customer needs.
2. **Implementation**:
    a. **AI Solutions**: Identify and implement AI tools and technologies that align with business goals and growth strategies.
    b. **Scalability Planning**: Develop a scalability plan that incorporates AI solutions to support future growth.
    c. **Continuous Improvement**: Monitor and refine AI implementations to ensure ongoing efficiency and effectiveness.

Conclusion

In this chapter, we explored how AI empowers entrepreneurs and small businesses to enhance their operations, improve customer relationships, and scale effectively. By leveraging AI automation, analytics, and personalization, businesses can streamline processes, make informed decisions, and deliver exceptional customer experiences. With the right AI tools and strategies, entrepreneurs can achieve sustainable growth and remain competitive in today's dynamic business landscape.

Chapter 8: Ethical Considerations and Challenges

Introduction

1. **The Importance of Ethics in AI**:
    a. **Overview**: As AI technology continues to advance, it is essential to consider the ethical implications and challenges associated with its use. Ensuring that AI applications are used responsibly and ethically is crucial for maintaining public trust and maximizing the benefits of AI.
    b. **Significance**: Ethical considerations help prevent misuse, promote fairness, and protect individual rights, which are critical for the sustainable development of AI technologies.

Ethical Use of AI

Ensuring Transparency and Fairness in AI Applications

1. **Transparency in AI**:
    a. **Definition**: Transparency in AI involves making the processes and decisions made by AI systems understandable and accessible to users and stakeholders.
    b. **Importance**:
        i. **Trust**: Builds trust between users and AI systems by providing clear explanations of how decisions are made.
        ii. **Accountability**: Enables accountability by allowing stakeholders to audit and understand AI decision-making processes.
    c. **Strategies for Ensuring Transparency**:
        i. **Explainable AI (XAI)**: Develop AI models that provide human-understandable explanations for their decisions and predictions.
        ii. **Documentation**: Maintain comprehensive documentation of AI models, including data sources, algorithms used, and decision-making processes.
        iii. **User Communication**: Clearly communicate how AI systems work and the rationale behind their outputs to users and stakeholders.
2. **Fairness in AI**:
    a. **Definition**: Fairness in AI involves ensuring that AI systems do not discriminate against individuals or groups and that their outputs are equitable.
    b. **Importance**:
        i. **Social Responsibility**: Prevents discrimination and promotes equality by addressing potential biases in AI systems.
        ii. **Legal Compliance**: Ensures compliance with anti-discrimination laws and regulations.
    c. **Strategies for Ensuring Fairness**:

      i. **Bias Detection and Mitigation**: Use techniques to identify and mitigate biases in AI algorithms and data.
      ii. **Diverse Data**: Ensure that training datasets are representative of diverse populations to minimize bias.
      iii. **Algorithmic Audits**: Regularly audit AI systems to detect and address any biases or unfair outcomes.

Addressing Biases in AI Systems

1. **Understanding AI Bias**:
   a. **Definition**: AI bias occurs when AI systems produce results that are systematically prejudiced due to biased data, algorithms, or design.
   b. **Types of Bias**:
      i. **Data Bias**: Arises from unrepresentative or skewed training data that reflects existing societal biases.
      ii. **Algorithmic Bias**: Occurs when AI algorithms amplify or perpetuate biases present in the data or design.
   c. **Impact**: Bias in AI systems can lead to unfair treatment of individuals or groups and undermine trust in AI technology.
2. **Strategies for Addressing AI Bias**:
   a. **Bias Evaluation**: Continuously evaluate AI systems for potential biases using statistical analysis and fairness metrics.
   b. **Inclusive Design**: Involve diverse teams in the design and development of AI systems to identify and address potential biases.
   c. **Bias Mitigation Techniques**: Implement techniques such as re-sampling, re-weighting, and algorithmic fairness interventions to reduce bias.

Data Privacy and Security

Protecting Sensitive Information in AI Applications

1. **Importance of Data Privacy**:
   a. **Definition**: Data privacy involves protecting personal and sensitive information from unauthorized access, use, or disclosure.
   b. **Significance**: Ensuring data privacy is essential for maintaining user trust and compliance with legal and regulatory requirements.
   c. **Challenges**:
      i. **Data Collection**: AI systems often require large amounts of data, raising concerns about how data is collected and used.
      ii. **Data Sharing**: Sharing data across organizations or systems can increase the risk of unauthorized access or misuse.
2. **Strategies for Protecting Data Privacy**:
   a. **Data Minimization**: Collect only the data necessary for the specific purpose of the AI application.
   b. **Anonymization and Encryption**: Use techniques to anonymize and encrypt data to protect sensitive information from unauthorized access.

c. **Access Controls**: Implement robust access controls and authentication measures to restrict access to sensitive data.

Compliance with Data Protection Regulations

1. **Key Data Protection Regulations**:
   a. **General Data Protection Regulation (GDPR)**: The European Union's GDPR sets strict guidelines for data protection and privacy.
   b. **California Consumer Privacy Act (CCPA)**: The CCPA provides California residents with rights regarding their personal information.
   c. **Other Regulations**: Numerous other countries and regions have enacted data protection laws to safeguard personal data.
2. **Strategies for Compliance**:
   a. **Data Protection Policies**: Develop and implement comprehensive data protection policies and procedures.
   b. **Data Subject Rights**: Ensure that individuals can exercise their rights, such as accessing their data or requesting its deletion.
   c. **Data Breach Response**: Establish a data breach response plan to address and mitigate the impact of data breaches.

Overcoming Common Challenges

Addressing Technical and Financial Barriers

1. **Technical Challenges**:
   a. **Complexity**: Developing and deploying AI systems can be complex and require specialized expertise.
   b. **Integration**: Integrating AI solutions into existing systems and processes can be challenging.
   c. **Scalability**: Scaling AI solutions to handle large volumes of data and transactions can pose technical challenges.
2. **Financial Challenges**:
   a. **Cost**: Implementing AI technology can be costly, requiring investment in infrastructure, software, and talent.
   b. **Resource Constraints**: Small businesses and startups may face resource constraints that limit their ability to invest in AI.
3. **Strategies for Overcoming Challenges**:
   a. **Partnerships and Collaboration**: Partner with AI vendors, research institutions, and other organizations to access expertise and resources.
   b. **Cloud-Based Solutions**: Leverage cloud-based AI services to reduce infrastructure costs and improve scalability.
   c. **Open Source Tools**: Utilize open-source AI tools and frameworks to reduce development costs.

Staying Updated with AI Advancements

1. **Continuous Learning and Adaptation**:

a. **Importance**: AI technology is rapidly evolving, and staying updated with advancements is essential for maintaining a competitive edge.
   b. **Challenges**:
      i. **Rapid Pace of Change**: The fast pace of AI advancements can make it difficult for businesses to keep up.
      ii. **Skill Gaps**: There may be a shortage of skilled professionals with expertise in the latest AI technologies.
2. **Strategies for Staying Updated**:
   a. **Training and Development**: Invest in training and development programs to upskill employees and keep them informed about the latest AI trends.
   b. **Industry Conferences and Workshops**: Attend industry conferences, workshops, and webinars to learn about new AI technologies and best practices.
   c. **Research and Innovation**: Foster a culture of research and innovation within the organization to explore new AI applications and opportunities.

Conclusion

In this chapter, we explored the ethical considerations and challenges associated with the use of AI in business. By ensuring transparency, fairness, and data privacy, businesses can build trust with customers and stakeholders while leveraging AI for innovation and growth. Overcoming technical and financial barriers and staying updated with AI advancements are essential for businesses to harness the full potential of AI technology responsibly and sustainably.

Conclusion

Recap of Key Strategies

Summarizing the Main Ways to Make Money with AI

1. **AI-Powered E-commerce**:
    a. **Enhancing Customer Experience**: Utilize AI for personalized recommendations and customer service automation.
    b. **Inventory Management**: Leverage predictive analytics for efficient stock management and supply chain automation.
    c. **Boosting Sales**: Implement dynamic pricing strategies and AI-driven marketing for increased sales.
2. **AI-Powered Side Hustles**:
    a. **Freelancing**: Use AI tools for graphic design, writing, and more to enhance productivity and creativity.
    b. **Creating and Selling AI Products**: Develop AI-driven apps and monetize AI-generated content like art and music.
    c. **Online Courses and Consulting**: Teach AI skills and offer consulting services for AI implementation.
3. **AI in Digital Marketing**:
    a. **Optimizing Marketing Campaigns**: Employ AI for audience segmentation and personalized messaging.
    b. **Content Creation and Curation**: Use AI tools for generating and curating high-quality content.
    c. **Social Media and Influencer Marketing**: Manage social media and identify influencers with AI.
4. **AI in Stock Market and Trading**:
    a. **Automated Trading Systems**: Set up AI-driven trading bots for efficient trading strategies.
    b. **Predictive Analytics for Investment**: Use AI to forecast market trends and manage risk.
    c. **Robo-Advisors**: Leverage AI-driven investment advisors for financial planning.
5. **AI in Real Estate**:
    a. **Property Valuation**: Use AI for accurate property assessments and market analysis.
    b. **Enhancing Property Management**: Implement AI for tenant screening and predictive maintenance.
    c. **Marketing Real Estate**: Utilize virtual tours and AI-enhanced property listings for targeted advertising.
6. **AI for Entrepreneurs and Small Businesses**:
    a. **Streamlining Operations**: Implement AI automation for operational efficiency.
    b. **Customer Relationship Management (CRM)**: Use AI-powered CRM systems for personalized customer interactions.

c. **Scaling Business**: Identify growth opportunities and scale operations with AI solutions.

Highlighting Actionable Steps for Getting Started

1. **Identify Opportunities**: Evaluate your business or personal skills to identify areas where AI can be applied for profit.
2. **Educate Yourself**: Learn about AI tools and technologies relevant to your interests or industry.
3. **Choose the Right Tools**: Select AI platforms and software that align with your goals and budget.
4. **Experiment and Iterate**: Start small by experimenting with AI solutions and iterating based on results.
5. **Network and Collaborate**: Join AI communities, attend conferences, and collaborate with experts to expand your knowledge and network.
6. **Monitor and Adapt**: Stay informed about AI advancements and continuously adapt your strategies to leverage new opportunities.

Future of AI and Profit Opportunities

Emerging Trends and Technologies

1. **AI and the Internet of Things (IoT)**:
   a. **Integration**: AI is increasingly being integrated with IoT devices, leading to smarter homes, cities, and industries.
   b. **Opportunities**: Explore opportunities in developing AI-driven IoT solutions for various sectors.
2. **AI in Healthcare**:
   a. **Advancements**: AI is transforming healthcare with applications in diagnostics, personalized medicine, and patient care.
   b. **Opportunities**: Consider opportunities in developing AI solutions for healthcare providers and patients.
3. **AI and Blockchain**:
   a. **Synergy**: The combination of AI and blockchain technologies is creating new opportunities for secure and transparent data management.
   b. **Opportunities**: Explore opportunities in developing AI-powered blockchain applications for finance, supply chain, and more.
4. **AI Ethics and Regulation**:
   a. **Importance**: As AI technology evolves, ethical considerations and regulations are becoming increasingly important.
   b. **Opportunities**: Engage in ethical AI development and compliance services to ensure responsible AI use.

Preparing for Future Opportunities in the AI Space

1. **Continuous Learning**: Stay updated with the latest AI research, trends, and technologies through courses, webinars, and industry publications.

2. **Embrace Innovation**: Foster a culture of innovation and experimentation to stay ahead in the rapidly evolving AI landscape.
3. **Focus on Sustainability**: Consider the environmental and social impact of AI solutions and strive for sustainable development.
4. **Adapt to Change**: Be agile and ready to adapt your strategies to new opportunities and challenges in the AI space.

Final Thoughts

The journey of making money with AI is filled with opportunities for innovation and growth. By leveraging AI technologies, entrepreneurs and businesses can enhance their operations, improve customer experiences, and explore new revenue streams. The key to success lies in continuous learning, ethical practices, and a willingness to adapt to the ever-changing AI landscape. Embrace the power of AI and embark on a transformative journey towards financial success and technological advancement.

Appendices

Glossary of AI Terms

Key AI Terms and Definitions

1. **Artificial Intelligence (AI)**: The simulation of human intelligence processes by machines, especially computer systems. This includes learning, reasoning, and self-correction.
2. **Machine Learning (ML)**: A subset of AI that involves the use of algorithms and statistical models to enable machines to improve their performance on a task through experience.
3. **Deep Learning**: A type of machine learning that uses neural networks with multiple layers (deep neural networks) to analyze and learn from large amounts of data.
4. **Neural Network**: A computational model inspired by the human brain, consisting of layers of interconnected nodes (neurons) that process data and learn patterns.
5. **Natural Language Processing (NLP)**: A branch of AI that focuses on the interaction between computers and humans through natural language, enabling machines to understand and generate human language.
6. **Computer Vision**: An area of AI that enables machines to interpret and make decisions based on visual data from the world.
7. **Algorithm**: A step-by-step procedure or formula for solving a problem or completing a task.
8. **Supervised Learning**: A type of machine learning where an algorithm is trained on labeled data, meaning the input data comes with the correct output.
9. **Unsupervised Learning**: A type of machine learning where the algorithm is trained on data without labels, and the system tries to learn the patterns and structure from the data.
10. **Reinforcement Learning**: A type of machine learning where an agent learns to make decisions by taking actions in an environment to achieve maximum cumulative reward.
11. **Big Data**: Extremely large data sets that may be analyzed computationally to reveal patterns, trends, and associations, especially relating to human behavior and interactions.
12. **Data Mining**: The practice of examining large databases to generate new information and discover patterns.
13. **Overfitting**: A modeling error in machine learning where a model learns the training data too well, capturing noise instead of the intended outputs.
14. **Bias**: In AI, bias refers to systematic errors in an AI system's output due to prejudiced assumptions made during the algorithm's development or the training data.
15. **Robo-Advisor**: An AI-driven financial advisor that provides automated, algorithm-based financial planning services without human intervention.

Resources and Further Reading

Books and Articles

1. **Books**:
    a. *Artificial Intelligence: A Guide to Intelligent Systems* by Michael Negnevitsky
    b. *Deep Learning* by Ian Goodfellow, Yoshua Bengio, and Aaron Courville
    c. *Superintelligence: Paths, Dangers, Strategies* by Nick Bostrom
2. **Articles and Papers**:
    a. "The AI Revolution: The Road to Superintelligence" by Tim Urban
    b. "The Malicious Use of Artificial Intelligence: Forecasting, Prevention, and Mitigation" by Brundage et al.

Websites and Online Courses

1. **Websites**:
    a. OpenAI
    b. Towards Data Science
    c. AI Trends
2. **Online Courses**:
    a. **Coursera**: Machine Learning by Andrew Ng
    b. **edX**: Artificial Intelligence MicroMasters by Columbia University
    c. **Udacity**: AI Programming with Python Nanodegree

Organizations and Communities

1. **Organizations**:
    a. **AI for Good**: An initiative by the International Telecommunication Union (ITU) to leverage AI for addressing global challenges.
    b. **Partnership on AI**: An organization that brings together academia, industry, and civil society to address AI-related challenges.
2. **Communities**:
    a. **AI Alignment Forum**: A community for discussing AI safety and alignment.
    b. **Kaggle**: A community of data scientists and machine learning practitioners.

Case Studies and Success Stories

AI in E-commerce

1. **Amazon's Recommendation System**:
    a. **Overview**: Amazon uses AI algorithms to analyze customer behavior and preferences to provide personalized product recommendations.
    b. **Impact**: The recommendation engine contributes significantly to Amazon's sales by enhancing the customer shopping experience.

2. **Alibaba's AI-Powered Customer Service**:
    a. **Overview**: Alibaba employs AI chatbots to handle customer inquiries, providing quick and efficient support.
    b. **Impact**: The AI-driven customer service system has improved customer satisfaction and reduced operational costs.

AI in Healthcare

1. **IBM Watson for Oncology**:
    a. **Overview**: IBM Watson uses AI to assist oncologists in identifying personalized treatment options for cancer patients.
    b. **Impact**: Watson for Oncology has helped healthcare providers make more informed decisions, improving patient outcomes.
2. **PathAI's Diagnostic Tool**:
    a. **Overview**: PathAI uses machine learning to assist pathologists in diagnosing diseases more accurately.
    b. **Impact**: The AI tool has improved diagnostic accuracy and efficiency, leading to better patient care.

AI in Finance

1. **JPMorgan Chase's Contract Intelligence (COiN)**:
    a. **Overview**: JPMorgan uses AI to automate the review and analysis of legal documents.
    b. **Impact**: COiN has reduced the time and cost associated with contract review, increasing operational efficiency.
2. **Betterment's Robo-Advisors**:
    a. **Overview**: Betterment provides AI-driven investment advice, offering personalized financial planning services.
    b. **Impact**: The robo-advisors have democratized access to financial advice, allowing individuals to manage investments effectively.

Templates and Tools for Implementing AI

AI Implementation Templates

1. **Project Planning Template**:
    a. **Purpose**: Helps outline objectives, timelines, and resources needed for AI projects.
    b. **Components**: Goals, scope, timeline, resource allocation, risk assessment, and success metrics.
2. **Data Collection and Preprocessing Template**:
    a. **Purpose**: Guides the collection, cleaning, and preprocessing of data for AI models.
    b. **Components**: Data sources, data cleaning steps, data transformation techniques, and data validation checks.

Tools for AI Development

1. **TensorFlow**:
    a. **Overview**: An open-source machine learning library developed by Google, used for building and deploying AI models.
    b. **Key Features**: Supports deep learning, neural networks, and large-scale machine learning applications.
2. **PyTorch**:
    a. **Overview**: An open-source machine learning library developed by Facebook, known for its flexibility and ease of use.
    b. **Key Features**: Dynamic computation graph, strong GPU acceleration, and a large community support.
3. **Scikit-Learn**:
    a. **Overview**: A Python library for simple and efficient tools for data mining and data analysis.
    b. **Key Features**: Easy integration with NumPy and pandas, wide range of algorithms, and excellent documentation.
4. **H2O.ai**:
    a. **Overview**: An open-source platform for AI and machine learning, offering automated machine learning (AutoML) tools.
    b. **Key Features**: User-friendly interface, supports R and Python, and scalability for big data applications.
5. **Google Cloud AI Platform**:
    a. **Overview**: A comprehensive AI platform that provides tools for building, deploying, and scaling AI models.
    b. **Key Features**: Integration with Google Cloud services, support for TensorFlow, and pre-built AI models.

Conclusion

The appendices section provides valuable resources and tools for readers to deepen their understanding of AI and its applications. By exploring the glossary, further reading materials, case studies, and practical templates, readers can enhance their knowledge and effectively implement AI solutions in their projects or businesses.